THE
NEXT GEN
ALMANAC

ALSO BY DREW Y. SANDERS

Finding Big Mo: A golf story
www.findingbigmo.com

Change Doesn't Bite: A story of a dog,
a team by the bay, and how to change your way
www.changedoesntbite.com

Branches & Roots Newsletter:
Released every 45 days
A look at strategy and competition through
the lens of business and sport.
www.banyantreestrategies.com/newsletters-blog
Coming Soon! www.branchesandroots.net

THE NEXT GEN ALMANAC

Helping You Track and Improve the Key Areas of Your Life

By Drew Y. Sanders and Sara H. Sanders

Foreword by Brigadier General Jeffrey W. Foley, MA, USA (Retired)

BANYAN TREE STRATEGIES

This book is dedicated to our amazing children, Ryan and Brooke, and to all those growing up in each "Next Gen" of the future.

TABLE OF CONTENTS

Foreword by Brig Gen Jeffrey W. Foley, MA, USA (Ret.)

Acknowledgements

Part I: Next Gen Almanac

Introduction... 3
Chapter 1: The Self Diagnosis Process 5
Chapter 2: Tips for Refueling Your Tank 13
Chapter 3: Working with a Coach/Mentor........... 25
Chapter 4: Worksheets 29

Part II: Growing Your Network - 50 Lunches a Year

Introduction... 33
Chapter 1: Changing Your Mindset................... 35
Chapter 2: Setting Up Your System.................. 39
Chapter 3: The Time of Year Makes a Difference... 43
Chapter 4: Your Lunch Why........................... 51
Chapter 5: Finally, the Meal........................... 55
Chapter 6: The Follow Up............................. 59

Appendix: Templates

1. 45 Day Worksheet
2. 45 Day Follow Up Questions
3. Wedding Cake Layers (2 pages)
4. Interesting Things Worksheet
5. Pre-Lunch Worksheet
6. Overall Task List
7. Prioritizing Tasks
8. Personal Goal and Behavior Sheet
9. Value Rank Contacts Sample
10. Mapping Your Boss

Foreword

I met Drew Sanders three years ago and have become fascinated with his incredible ability to teach and coach people. For decades, I have been impressed by those who can bring out the best in others through keen insight and techniques for inspiring change. Drew is at the top of the list.

Let's face it - life is complicated. Not enough time in the day to do all we want or need to get done. We get wrapped up in the agenda of others. We lose track of what we are doing for ourselves.

No matter how old or young, you have the opportunity to raise the bar on how you are living today and the legacy you leave. Whether you are a recent graduate, in a new business position, a new parent or grandparent, or even had a setback in your life - it is never too late to refocus on what you can change - *you*.

Successful people do not drift to greatness. They commit themselves to three things: learning, assessing where they are today, and taking action on a plan to focus on priorities. *The Next Gen Almanac* provides a practical, disciplined, powerful method for guiding you along this journey.

The catalyst for driving you to be the best you can be resides in your own heart and soul. This book can help you discover that catalyst and reignite your passion. We are fortunate to now have in writing what Drew and his wife, Sara, have been practicing for years. Give this book and its powerful lessons a chance. I believe it can really rock your world. It is that good!

Jeffrey W. Foley
Brigadier General, US Army (Retired)
Founder and CEO, Loral Mountain Solutions
Co-Author, *Rules and Tools for Leaders* (4th Edition)

Acknowledgements

We would like to extend a giant thank you to the friends and colleagues who took the time to read through our very rough first edition of The Next Gen Almanac and provide feedback about the content, style, details, and editing. Particularly we would like to thank Katy Orr, Jeff Hopper, and Jeffrey Foley, Brigadier General, US Army (Retired). We also greatly appreciate the feedback and time spent on reviewing and recommending changes from our gracious family and friends including Matt Flynn, Margaret Hallock, Jason Taormino, Joe Helmer, Laura Hazlett, Anthony Mosse, Todd Eichler, Kevin Kelly, Conrad Ray, Gary Aspiri, David Easthope, David Kearsley, Carolyn and John Sanders, and Steve De Luchi.

Many Thanks!

Drew and Sara Sanders

Part I

Your Dashboard for Success

How Full is Your Tank?

Introduction

Welcome to **The Next Gen Almanac**, your annual workbook for planning and living the best life you can imagine. As you turn your eyes towards a future filled with possibility and less school work, having a personal system in place to keep you focused and on track is crucial. But where are you going to get this system, your parents? The current younger generation will have a laugh at their parent's expense when they hear stories of email as a brand new communication tool, or the fax as an amazing invention. This has perhaps always been the case, but it has never been more impactful than in this era and time, with technologically driven disruptions across so many industries in a short span of time. Regardless of the innovations of the time, your parents probably also felt more advanced than *their* parents.

Being in your twenties is a time of "doing it your own way" and leading your generation into the future. Previous generations had the benefit of institutional structure, providing a way to organize their thoughts and action. Today, those structures no longer exist. Companies have never invested less in employees, and employees typically have returned that lack of investment by remaining in their jobs for shorter periods of time.

From the 1950's to the 1990's, corporations identified several tiers of college graduates and trained them accordingly. The last twenty years have seen a dismantling of corporate training departments. The result of this is a workforce of mid-40's professionals who have acquired skills on their own and they now expect you to do the same.

To help you navigate this gap, we offer you **The Next Gen Almanac**, a 52-week guide and workbook to help you keep a personal inventory of your vital systems and to provide a weekly process to follow. This book will help you focus on the right things at the right time. You will be able to implement this plan in 30 minutes each day, and each week it will take you 15 minutes to get re-centered.

The Next Gen Almanac is a tool to be shared with a coach or a manager so that you can be in total sync with the mentors in your life. It is a timeless truth that a personal relationship with your boss will have a significant impact on your overall job satisfaction.

Using **The Next Gen Almanac** to communicate with your leader on a weekly basis will increase your chances for a great relationship in three areas. First, it will show them you are organized: second, it will give them a window into how you think. Finally, using this tool will enable your mentor to direct you efficiently and effectively. Your goal is to position this person as your coach: a coach will always be invested in their committed and organized players.

We encourage you to make a commitment to invest 15 minutes a week toward monitoring your personal achievement process. The leaders of tomorrow are technologically flexible in all settings: they use the technology that is best for the job. A bound book is a time-tested piece of technology. A bound book will allow you to have a clear picture of how you performed last week, last month, or last year. As you use this system you will become more proficient and you will benefit from the ease of flipping back to a week in time and reading your own comments.

We challenge you to organize yourself each week, measure your tanks, and then execute your tasks with freedom and focus.

CHAPTER 1
The Self-Diagnosis Process

Think of your life as a series of areas that function like fuel tanks.
Like a car your optimal life should be possible if all your tanks are
full. Below, we've organized these tanks into a dashboard. The left
side of your dashboard represents your mind and body through the
soul and fuel gauges, and to some extent work. It measures your
personal overall health through your *inputs* in life and work. The
middle of your dashboard represents your *output* in the areas of
work, network, and fun, and specifically how those are filled related
to your interactions with others. The rightmost gauge connects you
into a broader spectrum of relations tied to community service.
Getting your internal systems in sync helps your outputs increase,
and your accomplishments fuel your feelings about yourself. Each
gauge of your dashboard can add fuel and balance to the other
areas, and they contribute in their own way to the stability and
healthiness of your overall self.

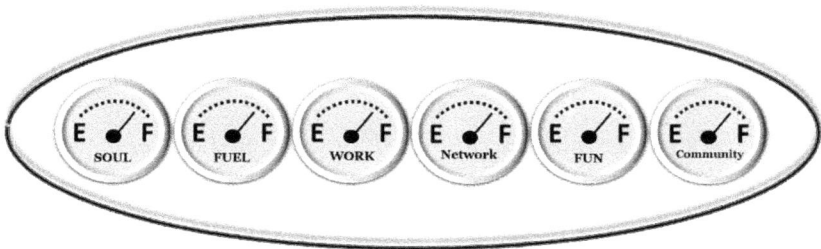

YOU   ALL

OTHERS

The SOUL Gauge

Most people when asked to define their soul will be at a loss for words. "What do you mean?" "How do I gauge that?" They don't want to get the question wrong. Is this a "God question?" "Are you asking about my faith?" This is actually not a big picture question. This is simply a quick inventory of how do you feel inside as it relates to three areas.

The first is your relationship with yourself. Do you feel right with yourself? The second is do you feel right and in sync with your most trusted relationships? And lastly, do you feel right and in sync with a higher power as you define it? Presented this way, it easy to rank how full your tank is in these areas. You are either feeling great about these areas, or you are not. This look in the mirror may not be easy, but it is actually one you can measure in seconds. Putting a mark on a gauge on a piece of paper forces you to address why you put it where you did. Try it for the first time here and fill in just one "to do" as an example:

- *Place an X on the dotted line for where your "tank" is right now*
- *Write in one "to do" to help fill the tank. Chapter 2 has some tips.*

SOUL	
Place an X on the "tanks" below	To fill the tank I need to:
Empty ----------------------Full **YOU**	1 2 3
Empty ----------------------Full **OTHERS**	1 2 3
Empty ----------------------Full **HIGHER POWER/NATURE**	1 2 3

The FUEL Gauge

Running your life engine requires that your mind and body be in sync. In this case your mind can be thought of as your mindset. These are the established set of attitudes you hold, the lens through which you look at your life. The long-term impact of your mindset should not be ignored, as it is a key lever in your life. You cannot ignore your mindset. Two other key levers are the food and liquids you put in your body, and the exercise you put your body through.

Typically, a young professional transitioning from school to work will notice a sharp decrease in free time, and along with that an increase in time sitting at a desk. This change can be a one-two punch to your overall health and fitness. Take a quick accounting in these three areas:

FUEL		
Place an X on the "tanks" below	To fill the tank I need to:	
Empty ----------------------Full **FOOD**	1 2 3	
Empty ----------------------Full **LIQUID & OTHER**	1 2 3	
Empty ----------------------Full **EXERCISE**	1 2 3	

The WORK Gauge

You now see how to keep your internal systems firing and in rhythm, so let's get your outputs up and running. Having a compelling narrative tied to a job or company you work with really matters. Your narrative is your story, the sound bites on why you are working at that company, and how it is matching your strengths and your vision. Regardless of your role at your company, you will want to track a few key metrics. Sharing these with your leader on a regular a basis will allow you to be in sync and is a proven way to stay on track for success. Peter Drucker, well known writer, professor, and management consultant, famously implored his followers to "seek performance, because without it there will be no advancement." Given the relaxed amount of corporate structure you are bound to face, having your own metrics graded on a weekly basis will serve you well.

Think about everyone at your company as an internal customer and then grade yourself on either how well you are perceived by them or how well you are serving them. This is your internal customer score. Next take a look at the role you are being asked to play, and now grade yourself on what is needed in this area. For example, if you are in sales, this would be your quota. If you are in engineering, it might be a quality assurance number. If you are in a support role, it may be if you contribute to making your boss or leader be more capable or proficient. Regardless of department you have a metric you can track. Combining these two grades can give you an all-work grade.

WORK	
Place an X on the "tanks" below	To fill the tank I need to:
Empty ----------------------Full **INTERNAL CUSTOMER**	1 2 3
Empty ----------------------Full **EXTERNAL CUSTOMER**	1 2 3

The NETWORK Gauge

Your life to this point has often been a series of experiences with others based upon the accomplishments of your parents. Your schooling, sports teams and science fairs have all been picked for you. Even your college which was "your choice" really had to be blessed by your great benefactors, i.e. your parents.

Looking ahead, you now have a lot more say in who you hang out with and what shared experiences you will have. This is often when you see just how soaring with the eagles vs running with the turkeys made a difference in your life to this point. Every shared experience you have now becomes an asset in your reputational bank account. The dividend that asset pays is directly tied to how accomplished the person is who is sharing thoughts about you. If the person extolling your strengths is accomplished, you will benefit.

Everyone owns their career, and most people want to grow what they own, but no one owns their reputation. It is in your best interest to be associated with the best group of people you can, and to get along with them while you are together. Once you are looking through this lens, you can see that regardless of your job, you choose who you eat and play with and these choices matter. Take a minute, gauge the following, and fill in not just a couple action items, but also whom you should spend more time with:

NETWORK	
Place an X on the "tanks" below	To fill the tank I need to:
Empty ----------------------Full **PEER GROUP**	1 2 3
Empty ----------------------Full **OLDER THAN YOU**	1 2 3
Empty ----------------------Full **YOUNGER THAN YOU**	1 2 3

The FUN Gauge

It may seem pointless to have a fun gauge, yet quickly tracking your fun will help you better understand what really is fun for you. Your available time for fun will become much smaller as you age, so maybe that trip to Vegas that takes a week to recover from is not really as fun as it used to be. Then again, if you love that trip and can't imagine missing the event, then that will come out in this process as well. We have broken up the gauge into two areas, fun alone and fun with others, to help you analyze and allocate time for yourself if, like many people, you truly refuel when you are alone or in a very small group.

FUN	
Place an X on the "tanks" below	To fill the tank I need to:
Empty ----------------------Full **FUN ALONE**	1 2 3
Empty ----------------------Full **FUN WITH OTHERS**	1 2 3

The COMMUNITY SERVICE Gauge

Committing to a cause greater than oneself is one of the secrets for success that many people miss while they are getting through the high-stress education years. Helping others is contagious in the best of ways, and it really can help you build out your executive tool kit in the process. Opportunities to help your community abound, and the quickest way to identify what you should do is to ask yourself the following question:

> *Where do your strengths and interests match a need in your community?*

Are you a natural teacher and coach? Then find a youth sports league and volunteer coach. Are you really good with numbers? Then volunteer as a treasurer for a nonprofit that speaks to your heart. Are you good with your hands? Then find a Habitat for Humanity type of project and grab a hammer.

As you begin to "pitch in", watch as your network of influential people skyrockets. A huge side benefit of helping others is meeting all the like-minded people who have their life organized enough to give back. Once you are serving side-by-side, that shared experience will have a lifetime value that is highly sought after and seldom found at work. The message here is simple: get organized and get involved, and while serving others watch for the many opportunities that come your way.

COMMUNITY SERVICE	
Place an X on the "tanks" below	To fill the tank I need to:
Empty ----------------------Full **CAUSE 1**	1 2 3
Empty ----------------------Full **CAUSE 2**	1 2 3

Notes:

Chapter 2
Tips to Help You Refuel Your Tanks

As you venture into and get comfortable using **The Next Gen Almanac** worksheets on the following pages, we want to give you some tips and prompts for filling up your tanks if some are low. Use the next few pages as a reference guide to give you a quick start on filling back up. Maybe a word or key phrase will fire you up or get you thinking in a different way to help plug your leak.

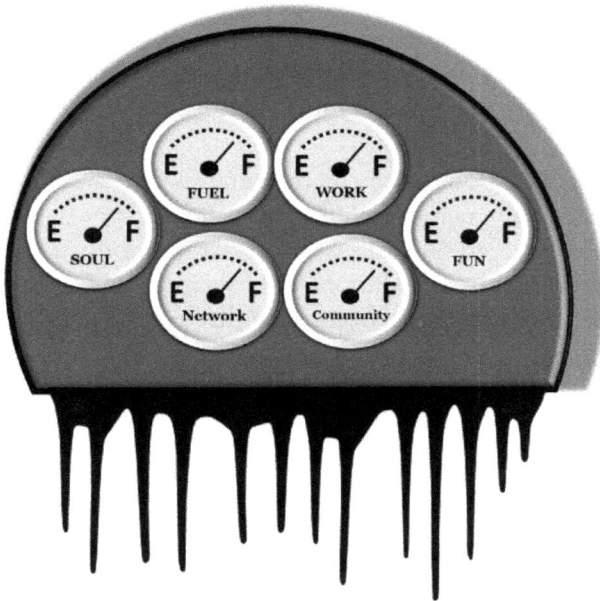

SOUL

You

- **Create some quiet time**

Dr. Glen Albaugh, a sports psychologist, friend, and mentor, often says "If you never make time for quiet, you will never have quiet time." This has really stuck with us over the years: quiet time is something we don't prioritize enough. Turn off all your media and go for a walk, or find a quiet corner where you live. Let your mind settle.

- **Reflective writing**

Sometimes it is hard to start, but you will often find it is then hard to stop. You don't have to show anybody what you write, but the worst conversations are the ones in your head. Getting them out on paper helps. Hand written notes to people you interact with are also important and are becoming a rarity, try to write several per month.

- **Read**

Pick up that book you have been meaning to start and take a break. Have an electronic memo wish list on your smartphone for books that you want to read on various topics. Without this you will notice interesting books mentioned across media, friends, and publications, but then later forget the title.

- **Breathing**

You will be surprised what taking a few minutes for some heart-centered, focused, long breaths can do to help you relax. Try it at least a few times a day, for more help here go to www.heartmap.com.

Others

- **Open up to others**

Be curious, be patient. Realize that your body language and non-verbal communication is important. You may have grown up in a texting and email world, and it is key to engage with others in a way that makes them know you are authentic. This starts with your shoulders; square them to your audience. Your eyes matter significantly as well, keep them up and, if possible, maintain an open face.

- **Listen**

Really listen until people are done talking. This is very hard but gets easier with practice. Let them finish and ask yourself, why is this person saying this now?

- **Draw a bigger circle**

See the bigger picture, look at all the factors going into every situation. This dovetails with asking why are you listening above. Learn to look for the context in the communication.

- **Learn their love languages**

This is from a popular book "The Five Love Languages", by Dr. Gary Chapman, but it is not just helpful for couples. When you realize the different ways we each express ourselves (such as, acts of service vs. quality time) a lot of frustration can be alleviated. The key here is empathy towards others. As others see you connect to their needs, their interest in you will increase. This norm of reciprocity is a life blood for teams.

Higher Power / Nature

- **Pray, worship, sing**

These can all go together and are very personal. This doesn't have to happen in a religious context, but it's an important one for any means to center yourself. You can do this alone or in an appropriate setting.

- **Visit religious/spiritual facility**

Been meaning to go to your church or other place of worship or spirituality, and just haven't gotten around to it? Make it a priority, or visit a website or watch some YouTube videos and see how it resonates with you.

FUEL

Food

- **Meal plan and time of day**

Having a plan for what you will eat every day – and what time you will eat -- can do a lot for your mood and well-being. This is often something that falls by the wayside. Even planning to have snacks with you is helpful.

- **Have a restaurant game plan**

Along with a meal plan comes being organized with meals out or business meals. As we detail in Part II of this book, maintaining a healthy diet can be aided by choosing familiar restaurants that you know have healthy options.

- **Water**

Most people underestimate the importance of drinking enough water. Get a refillable jug and commit to drinking a certain amount every day. The difference will amaze you.

There are some really fantastic apps on the market for helping with food intake and planning. Take a few minutes and research ones that may be helpful for you.

Alcohol, coffee, et. al

By fluids we mostly mean alcohol. Is your tank low because you imbibe too often? Ask yourself some of these tough questions:

- **Is it social drinking?**

Try sticking to a set number of drinks and sip your way there.

- **Who are your enablers?**

Try asking them for help to curtail or lessen the amount or try taking a break from certain groups.

- **Have a pre-planned reason for drinking alcohol**

Don't drink just because: have a reason (a party) and plan ahead, just like with food.

Exercise

- **Average the last three weeks of workouts**

Are you being consistent, or are you happy with the average? How about with the variety and duration?

- **Pre-plan the time to work out**

It has to be scheduled or you will find a reason not to do it.

- **Enter a race**

It's become trendy to do all kinds of races, skilled or not, slow or fast. There have never been more opportunities. So break out of your daily routine and train for a race, or just to meet a particular goal (e.g. seven-minute mile). It is always helpful to have something to shoot for, whether it is just walking five miles or doing a triathlon.

Notes:

_____

_____

_____

_____

_____

_____

_____

_____

_____

_____

WORK

Internal

- **Listen**

In many work environments your co-workers make up a very important customer base for you. Where you rank in their minds when it comes to effectiveness and trustworthiness can have a significant impact on your peer review scores. When others are talking, see if you can pick up why they are communicating along with what they are saying. As you improve in this area, it will start to impact how others treat you as once someone feels heard they typically start to trust you.

- **Observe others**

Now that you are working on your ability to listen in two ways, see if you can start to observe others non-verbal communication cues. Leadership is often associated with knowing what needs to come next before others do. A big part of this can come from experience, but if you don't have experience in a certain role, you can make up for it by your powers of observation that are the building blocks for maximizing your contribution to the group.

External

- **Distraction quotient (DQ)**

Measuring your DQ can be a game changer for the fully connected worker. Text messages, email alerts, and ring tones may make you feel like you on "on the job", but the higher up you go in a company the more you are going to be paid to think. Analyze the type of work you are being asked to perform and then start to realize how much sustained thought is required. Multi-tasking has been proven to be a myth. Your brain is actually switching back and forth at light speeds which can feel invigorating, yet it in most work environments you lose a dose of effectiveness with each switch. Ask yourself, in a competitive environment, can you spare the loss?

- **Delegate it**

When you were in school, turning in someone else's work is grounds for dismissal. When you lead a work team that is essentially what you are doing. Take a look at your tasks, prioritize what needs to be done and then see if you can leverage your time by outsourcing your low value tasks. Virtual assistants abound and work share sites like www.upwork.com allow you to start working like an manager much earlier than most of us ever thought possible even 10 years ago. Check with your boss, but as fast as you can, learn how to delegate and monitor for success. It is your future.

Key Performance Indicators (KPI)

In business, if it can't be measured, it is often forgotten. In your new career, if you think you are working hard and want recognition but don't have something to show that can be measured, then you are asking for a favor. Those are hard to come by. You are better off demanding a measurement to track, and then marshaling your resources to move that measurement.

- **Identify your Big Rock**

Once you have come to an accord with your boss about your KPI, clear the decks and deliver. Make sure to understand how your tasks blend with those around you to make your overall unit perform. Combining a laser focus on your deliverable, while not losing sight of those around you, will make you indispensable to your team and your boss. Whenever possible, keep your big rocks to less than 3 items. Having only one is preferred.

- **Identify how to communicate with leaders and direct reports**

Do you understand the personalities of those on your work team? Do you need to do a refresh on how to work with them? Look for our "Mapping Your Boss" worksheet in the appendix.

Notes:

NETWORK

Peers

- **Fifty Lunches idea**

Part II of the book we outline how to have 50 lunches a year to increase your network

- **Three to six-week calendar**

Try segmenting your calendar into chunks to better organize your objectives. Look in our appendix for some 45-day templates.

- **Make a modern day paper route**

Establish a routine for regular communication to your network so you don't lose touch with valuable allies and friends.

Older than you

- **Seek guidance and coaching/mentoring**

It is a great idea to reach out to those older to ask for some mentoring or advice: most are flattered and happy to help. Our mentoring definition is that you do 99% of the work and they offer 1%, with perspective and guidance on your efforts.

- **Identify potential sponsors**

Do you have a clear idea of those older folks that are your biggest fans and supporters? Have a short list to call on if you need a sponsor.

Younger than you

- **Help provide connections**

Look for younger folks who you can mentor or provide coaching to when asked. This usually comes back as a benefit or key connection down the road.

- **Get asked in**

Invite people into your network, don't corner them with an assessment or critique. It is easy to pass judgement on those younger, instead ask them to be a part of your future and be a mentor.

FUN

By yourself

- **Big Trip**

Afraid to travel and try something by yourself? Do it! You will have to meet people along the way, or spend quality time with your own thoughts.

- **Different experience**

Don't get stuck in a rut at a young age. Try something new or make a realistic bucket list, and put it on your wall.

- **Personal challenge**

Write down a personal challenge and specify some timeframes and goals. Keep those written goals in front of you, at your desk or a place you'll see it every day.

- **Life Goals**

Start writing down everything you want in life, no matter how unrealistic or small. After 100 items, start organizing by category.

With others

- **Teamwork idea**

Organize a function with workers or friends, or plan a lunch every 90 days. Pick an event to rally the troops. Become a social leader, meaning not always a meet up at a bar but organizing outings like theater, golf, or picnics. If this idea makes you cringe, identify the people in your network who love to do this, and offer to help them in a comfortable style for you.

COMMUNITY SERVICE

Causes

- **Build out a new skill set and cross train**

Are your causes something you could do more for if you had a different skill to offer? "Success comes in terms of relationships. Success is measured by the impact you make on other people's lives. And I think the second criterion is that all of us ought to have some kind of cause, some kind of purpose in our lives that's bigger than our own individual hopes, dreams, wants and desires. Life's about relationships and having a cause bigger than yourself. Simple as that." - *Peter Drucker*

- **Can it tie you to the community?**

Do your causes help tie you to your community? Are you meeting more people in your community or helping your community directly? Pitching in to help a larger group of people has shown to be a true win-win, especially if you have recently moved. You will meet people who have a similar sense of duty and in a few months you will feel comfortable seeing faces you recognize. These shared experiences will allow you to work on new areas in your skill development, and allow others to be a reference to your character.

- **Sense of connection**

Find a cause that gives you a sense of community or of being a part of something bigger than yourself. As we learned from Joe Ehrmann, author of *InsideOut Coaching* and founder of *Coach For America*, it's not enough to have an opinion and a commitment to a cause greater than yourself without turning thought into action.

Ehrmann challenges all of us to take our efforts to the next level. A very simple way to teach the lesson of enacting justice on behalf of others is to institute the lunchroom rule, which is to not let anyone sit alone at a meal. Invite the person to sit with you, with the team, with your friends. Think of how difficult it must be for someone to be alone. Empathize with them and put yourself in their shoes. Stand up for those weaker than you, those with less than you, those struggling and down. As Dr. Martin Luther King said, "A threat to justice anywhere is a threat to justice everywhere."

Chapter 3
Working with a Coach/Mentor or Asking for Help from an Expert

Now that you can peg how full your tanks are and have written down your action steps for improvement, the next thing to learn is how to share this information with a trusted mentor or coach. This is a vital step in your process as it helps you declare your intention both to yourself and to someone else. The act of the declaration will help cement your determination to improve. This dash of "peer pressure" can work in your favor and has been a key element of team building for years.

Tips for selecting your coach
Pick out a few people you really admire and then see if you can get a 1% commitment out of them to coach you. Laying out the ground rules is vital for this to work and we have found that the 1% rule can really make a difference. We suggest you layout what you would like their help with, and then say you will do 99% of the work, asking them to direct you, which is the missing 1%.

Your pitch
"I respect you and was curious if I might ask that you review my efforts from time to time. Your perspective and guidance will be extremely valuable to me, and I will be doing 99% of the work and ask that you would be able to review my efforts in 10-15 minutes and then share your thoughts over a cup of coffee, when time permits.

"My current goal is to accomplish the following, and I would love to include you in my process towards that goal. Getting your coaching on an infrequent basis would be an honor and I really appreciate your consideration."

Why this works
Several things are going on when you reach out to someone with this type of offer. First, you are telling them that they are respected; and this is a major deposit in their emotional bank account. Second,

you are defining the terms of the engagement, which lets the person know that you are not going to be a drain on a valuable life asset, their time. By outlining your steps and limiting the scope of their time to 45 minutes every month or so, you are making it really easy for them to say yes. Finally, when you share these templates with them you will show them just how organized you are, and they will be more inclined to jump in and assist you. Everyone wants to coach a future leader.

Can you have multiple coaches?

Yes, but there is a point of diminishing returns. If you start something you need to finish it, or else this person of great influence will think you are someone who doesn't keep their commitments. Your fifth grade teacher taught you that turning in your homework matters, so make sure you can deliver.

Turning your boss into your coach

Along with your outside work coaches, the person you most want to buy into your future is your boss. In a perfect world, your boss would have a process like this in place already, and you two would get in sync immediately. The fact is that your boss is trying to figure out their boss, and really would just love it if you did your job and didn't cause any problems.

Understanding what makes your boss tick, how they learn, and how they make decisions, as discussed earlier, is important, and also referenced in a worksheet at the end of the appendix. What you want to establish is a regular rhythm of communication where they can take off their taskmaster hat and put on their coach hat. The templates included in this book will allow you to share what you are thinking on your key performance indicators (KPI's) for work, and make it easier for your boss to coach you on how to improve. Bosses will always have opinions, but it is up to you to tease the advice out of them.

Getting your coaching staff assembled

Most high-performing professionals or athletes have a series of advisers that help them in different key areas of their life. Why should you be any different? Use these templates and our gauges to work effectively with your key influencers and then turn them in to your coaches. It has been our experience that, when approached correctly and treated with respect, everyone loves to be called "Coach". Think about your dream team of coaches. Who are they? What is stopping you from asking for their help? Once compiled, you will have a group of people invested in your progress, and that will include your boss. Now all that is left is monitoring your gauges, and staying in sync with your team. It feels great to be coached by people who are experts and who care about your success.

Notes:

Chapter 4 – Worksheets

The following pages contain six weeks of Next Gen worksheets for you to fill out (each worksheet is two pages).

There are additional helpful templates in the Appendix.

The Next Gen Almanac Worksheet

How Full is Your Tank?

NAME:

DATE:

SOUL

Place an X on the "tanks" below	To Fill the tank I need to:
YOU: EMPTY-----------------------------------FULL	1 2 3
OTHERS: EMPTY-----------------------------------FULL	1 2 3
HIGHER POWER / NATURE: EMPTY-----------------------------------FULL	1 2 3

FUEL

Place an X on the "tanks" below	To Fill the tank I need to:
FOOD: EMPTY-----------------------------------FULL	1 2 3
LIQUIDS: EMPTY-----------------------------------FULL	1 2 3
EXERCISE: EMPTY-----------------------------------FULL	1 2 3

WORK

Place an X on the "tanks" below	To Fill the tank I need to:
INTERNAL: EMPTY-----------------------------------FULL	1 2 3
EXTERNAL: EMPTY-----------------------------------FULL	1 2 3
KEY PERFORMANCE INDICATOR (KPI) EMPTY-----------------------------------FULL	1 2 3

NETWORKING

Place an X on the "tanks" below	To Fill the tank I need to:
PEERS: EMPTY----------------------------------FULL	1 2 3
OLDER: EMPTY----------------------------------FULL	1 2 3
YOUNGER: EMPTY----------------------------------FULL	1 2 3

FUN

Place an X on the "tanks" below	To Fill the tank I need to:
ALONE: EMPTY----------------------------------FULL	1 2 3
WITH OTHERS: EMPTY----------------------------------FULL	1 2 3

COMMUNITY SERVICE

Place an X on the "tanks" below	To Fill the tank I need to:
CAUSE 1: EMPTY----------------------------------FULL	1 2 3
CAUSE 2: EMPTY----------------------------------FULL	1 2 3

FOLLOW UP QUESTIONS

What is your most crucial gauge right now?	What are the top 3 things on your "Fill the Tank" list? "Fill the tank" list?
	1
Why?	2
	3

The Next Gen Almanac Worksheet

How Full is Your Tank?

NAME:

DATE:

SOUL

Place an X on the "tanks" below		To Fill the tank I need to:
YOU: EMPTY----------------------------------FULL	1 2 3	
OTHERS: EMPTY----------------------------------FULL	1 2 3	
HIGHER POWER / NATURE: EMPTY----------------------------------FULL	1 2 3	

FUEL

Place an X on the "tanks" below		To Fill the tank I need to:
FOOD: EMPTY----------------------------------FULL	1 2 3	
LIQUIDS: EMPTY----------------------------------FULL	1 2 3	
EXERCISE: EMPTY----------------------------------FULL	1 2 3	

WORK

Place an X on the "tanks" below		To Fill the tank I need to:
INTERNAL: EMPTY----------------------------------FULL	1 2 3	
EXTERNAL: EMPTY----------------------------------FULL	1 2 3	
KEY PERFORMANCE INDICATOR (KPI) EMPTY----------------------------------FULL	1 2 3	

NETWORKING

Place an X on the "tanks" below	To Fill the tank I need to:
PEERS: EMPTY----------------------------------FULL	1 2 3
OLDER: EMPTY----------------------------------FULL	1 2 3
YOUNGER: EMPTY----------------------------------FULL	1 2 3

FUN

Place an X on the "tanks" below	To Fill the tank I need to:
ALONE: EMPTY----------------------------------FULL	1 2 3
WITH OTHERS: EMPTY----------------------------------FULL	1 2 3

COMMUNITY SERVICE

Place an X on the "tanks" below	To Fill the tank I need to:
CAUSE 1: EMPTY----------------------------------FULL	1 2 3
CAUSE 2: EMPTY----------------------------------FULL	1 2 3

FOLLOW UP QUESTIONS

What is your most crucial gauge right now?	What are the top 3 things on your "Fill the Tank" list? "Fill the tank" list?
	1
Why?	2
	3

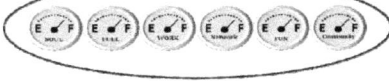

The Next Gen Almanac Worksheet
How Full is Your Tank?

NAME:

DATE:

SOUL	
Place an X on the "tanks" below	To Fill the tank I need to:
YOU: EMPTY----------------------------------FULL	1 2 3
OTHERS: EMPTY----------------------------------FULL	1 2 3
HIGHER POWER / NATURE: EMPTY----------------------------------FULL	1 2 3

FUEL	
Place an X on the "tanks" below	To Fill the tank I need to:
FOOD: EMPTY----------------------------------FULL	1 2 3
LIQUIDS: EMPTY----------------------------------FULL	1 2 3
EXERCISE: EMPTY----------------------------------FULL	1 2 3

WORK	
Place an X on the "tanks" below	To Fill the tank I need to:
INTERNAL: EMPTY----------------------------------FULL	1 2 3
EXTERNAL: EMPTY----------------------------------FULL	1 2 3
KEY PERFORMANCE INDICATOR (KPI) EMPTY----------------------------------FULL	1 2 3

NETWORKING

Place an X on the "tanks" below	To Fill the tank I need to:
PEERS: EMPTY----------------------------------FULL	1 2 3
OLDER: EMPTY----------------------------------FULL	1 2 3
YOUNGER: EMPTY----------------------------------FULL	1 2 3

FUN

Place an X on the "tanks" below	To Fill the tank I need to:
ALONE: EMPTY----------------------------------FULL	1 2 3
WITH OTHERS: EMPTY----------------------------------FULL	1 2 3

COMMUNITY SERVICE

Place an X on the "tanks" below	To Fill the tank I need to:
CAUSE 1: EMPTY----------------------------------FULL	1 2 3
CAUSE 2: EMPTY----------------------------------FULL	1 2 3

FOLLOW UP QUESTIONS

What is your most crucial gauge right now?	What are the top 3 things on your "Fill the Tank" list? "Fill the tank" list?
	1
Why?	2
	3

The Next Gen Almanac Worksheet
How Full is Your Tank?

NAME:

DATE:

SOUL

Place an X on the "tanks" below		To Fill the tank I need to:
YOU: **EMPTY**------------------------------------**FULL**	1 2 3	
OTHERS: **EMPTY**------------------------------------**FULL**	1 2 3	
HIGHER POWER / NATURE: **EMPTY**------------------------------------**FULL**	1 2 3	

FUEL

Place an X on the "tanks" below		To Fill the tank I need to:
FOOD: **EMPTY**------------------------------------**FULL**	1 2 3	
LIQUIDS: **EMPTY**------------------------------------**FULL**	1 2 3	
EXERCISE: **EMPTY**------------------------------------**FULL**	1 2 3	

WORK

Place an X on the "tanks" below		To Fill the tank I need to:
INTERNAL: **EMPTY**------------------------------------**FULL**	1 2 3	
EXTERNAL: **EMPTY**------------------------------------**FULL**	1 2 3	
KEY PERFORMANCE INDICATOR (KPI) **EMPTY**------------------------------------**FULL**	1 2 3	

NETWORKING	
Place an X on the "tanks" below	To Fill the tank I need to:
PEERS: EMPTY----------------------------------FULL	1 2 3
OLDER: EMPTY----------------------------------FULL	1 2 3
YOUNGER: EMPTY----------------------------------FULL	1 2 3

FUN	
Place an X on the "tanks" below	To Fill the tank I need to:
ALONE: EMPTY----------------------------------FULL	1 2 3
WITH OTHERS: EMPTY----------------------------------FULL	1 2 3

COMMUNITY SERVICE	
Place an X on the "tanks" below	To Fill the tank I need to:
CAUSE 1: EMPTY----------------------------------FULL	1 2 3
CAUSE 2: EMPTY----------------------------------FULL	1 2 3

FOLLOW UP QUESTIONS

What is your most crucial gauge right now?	What are the top 3 things on your "Fill the Tank" list? "Fill the tank" list?
	1
Why?	2
	3

The Next Gen Almanac Worksheet
How Full is Your Tank?

NAME:

DATE:

SOUL

Place an X on the "tanks" below		To Fill the tank I need to:
YOU: EMPTY------------------------------------FULL	1 2 3	
OTHERS: EMPTY------------------------------------FULL	1 2 3	
HIGHER POWER / NATURE: EMPTY------------------------------------FULL	1 2 3	

FUEL

Place an X on the "tanks" below		To Fill the tank I need to:
FOOD: EMPTY------------------------------------FULL	1 2 3	
LIQUIDS: EMPTY------------------------------------FULL	1 2 3	
EXERCISE: EMPTY------------------------------------FULL	1 2 3	

WORK

Place an X on the "tanks" below		To Fill the tank I need to:
INTERNAL: EMPTY------------------------------------FULL	1 2 3	
EXTERNAL: EMPTY------------------------------------FULL	1 2 3	
KEY PERFORMANCE INDICATOR (KPI) EMPTY------------------------------------FULL	1 2 3	

NETWORKING

Place an X on the "tanks" below	To Fill the tank I need to:
PEERS: **EMPTY**-----------------------------------**FULL**	1 2 3
OLDER: **EMPTY**-----------------------------------**FULL**	1 2 3
YOUNGER: **EMPTY**-----------------------------------**FULL**	1 2 3

FUN

Place an X on the "tanks" below	To Fill the tank I need to:
ALONE: **EMPTY**-----------------------------------**FULL**	1 2 3
WITH OTHERS: **EMPTY**-----------------------------------**FULL**	1 2 3

COMMUNITY SERVICE

Place an X on the "tanks" below	To Fill the tank I need to:
CAUSE 1: **EMPTY**-----------------------------------**FULL**	1 2 3
CAUSE 2: **EMPTY**-----------------------------------**FULL**	1 2 3

FOLLOW UP QUESTIONS

What is your most crucial gauge right now?	What are the top 3 things on your "Fill the Tank" list? "Fill the tank" list?
	1
Why?	2
	3

The Next Gen Almanac Worksheet
How Full is Your Tank?

NAME:

DATE:

SOUL

Place an X on the "tanks" below	To Fill the tank I need to:
YOU: EMPTY-----------------------------------FULL	1 2 3
OTHERS: EMPTY-----------------------------------FULL	1 2 3
HIGHER POWER / NATURE: EMPTY-----------------------------------FULL	1 2 3

FUEL

Place an X on the "tanks" below	To Fill the tank I need to:
FOOD: EMPTY-----------------------------------FULL	1 2 3
LIQUIDS: EMPTY-----------------------------------FULL	1 2 3
EXERCISE: EMPTY-----------------------------------FULL	1 2 3

WORK

Place an X on the "tanks" below	To Fill the tank I need to:
INTERNAL: EMPTY-----------------------------------FULL	1 2 3
EXTERNAL: EMPTY-----------------------------------FULL	1 2 3
KEY PERFORMANCE INDICATOR (KPI) EMPTY-----------------------------------FULL	1 2 3

NETWORKING

Place an X on the "tanks" below	To Fill the tank I need to:
PEERS: EMPTY-----------------------------------FULL	1 2 3
OLDER: EMPTY-----------------------------------FULL	1 2 3
YOUNGER: EMPTY-----------------------------------FULL	1 2 3

FUN

Place an X on the "tanks" below	To Fill the tank I need to:
ALONE: EMPTY-----------------------------------FULL	1 2 3
WITH OTHERS: EMPTY-----------------------------------FULL	1 2 3

COMMUNITY SERVICE

Place an X on the "tanks" below	To Fill the tank I need to:
CAUSE 1: EMPTY-----------------------------------FULL	1 2 3
CAUSE 2: EMPTY-----------------------------------FULL	1 2 3

FOLLOW UP QUESTIONS

What is your most crucial gauge right now?	What are the top 3 things on your "Fill the Tank" list? "Fill the tank" list? 1
Why?	2 3

Part II

Growing Your Network

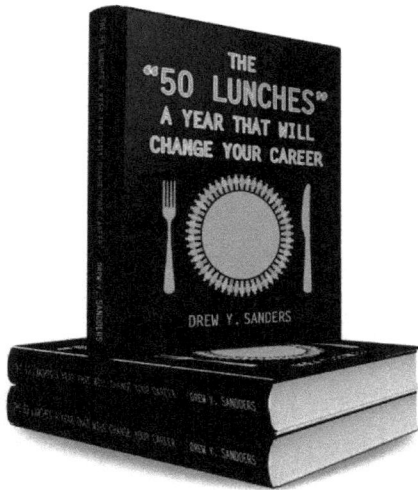

Fifty Lunches a Year

That Could Change Your Career

Introduction

How are you going to grow your influence and your career? What is your plan? Our research shows most people don't have a plan and get stuck worrying about whether or not their boss has a favorable opinion of them. Keeping your boss happy is a good idea, but we would like to suggest that you deploy an additional strategy. We believe you can expand and grow your career by establishing a simple plan of having one lunch a week with someone in your network of contacts.

In this part II, we will share with you how to set up your schedule, whom to invite, and when to invite them. We will also discuss where you should go to lunch and then dive into the details of the lunch itself. Finally, we will share how you should follow up after the lunch. I honed this knowledge over a ten-year period where I averaged 125 lunches a year, with a few lessons learned along the way. Your career is your own and it helps to have a wide and diverse set of people to work with to grow it. We also found that in general the hard truth is people don't care about your career, they care about their own career. Until you sit down with someone and talk about their personal career plans, they won't care about your career. So how are you going to grow the number of people who care about your career when you are eating lunch at your desk?

Going to lunch with a friend or colleague seems easy enough, and yet the data suggests most of us eat with the same people and don't expand our networks over lunch. Why should you care about this? Most of us are going to have working careers of some sort for almost 50 years. If that is the case, then it might be a good idea to get out of the building and meet some of those people you are commuting with.

Think about it: if you worked 250 days last year, how many times did you miss lunch? How many times did you not eat between 10:30 am and 2:30 pm, Monday through Friday? Chances are you did eat, either at your desk or at the company cafeteria, or you grabbed a quick sandwich somewhere close.

Consider that it is often not the smartest practitioner who has the largest practice or the most influence. It is the combination of competency and relationships that make a difference. The ability to build and cultivate strong relationships across a diverse geographic and professional landscape is critical. While this is not breaking news to most professionals, few knowledge workers have a system in place for building their professional network. A lack of time is the common lament for most and yet right in the middle of the day sits a key relationship-building event: **lunch**.

How many people can you feed in a network? What are your current time constraints or habits? Can they be changed? It's up to you to be authentic.
Metcalfe's Law Reigns

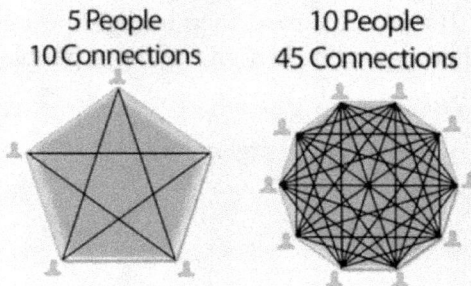

Metcalfe's Law

5 People
10 Connections

10 People
45 Connections

Chapter 1
Changing Your Mindset

If you are like most people, you most likely live 15 to 60 minutes away from work. Your home network or social structure may be diverse and wonderful. However, the context of those relationships is driven by family and community initiatives. Being "Bobby Business" at the softball game could have people running for the dugouts. Home is not always the ideal place to build your career.

Turning our attention back to the workplace, let's look at your day. You arrive for work and fulfill your role for the company and work on your assigned tasks. Your mind and your stomach feel the lunch bell ringing and you satisfy the need for sustenance. You return to your desk and plow forward until it is time to commute home. Your day may have plenty of meetings, webinars, and phone calls, but your number of contacts isn't growing.

If you work in a metropolitan area, as the majority of all knowledge workers do, you are spending eight to ten hours in a geographically dense area with similar professionals who all eat their mid-day meal at about the same time. Most of your fellow professionals have budgets, goals and initiatives that they are working towards. Most goals involve people. Yet day after day most professionals eat lunch, alone. Why?

In interviewing hundreds of professionals, we have learned that the biggest issue is a lack of time, followed by a secondary concern that the return on the investment of time is unclear. In short, the non-tactical lunch is considered a luxury.

> *Digging a little deeper, what we found was that professionals have plenty of time to eat a 45-minute lunch with a colleague; it's the time it takes to set up the lunch that most people misallocate.*

We further found that adding in a pre-set date and time for lunch increased the chances that a person went to lunch with another person. We will show you how to slightly adjust your calendar, your contacts, and your schedule so that you can fit in one lunch a week that, over time, will hopefully help you add breadth and depth to your business network.

It is one hour a week, but is it worth it?
For the skeptic, we cannot promise that the 1.25 hours you put in to the lunch each week will give you the maximum ROI versus eating lunch at your desk while you keep emailing and checking the water cooler. However, we would like share a personal story that we hope emboldens those on the fence to take the leap and ask someone to lunch.

For the past ten years I have been going to lunch with people as a way to get to know them better and then seeing if we can help each other. Whatever could happen over a meal I have probably seen it; sauce on the tie, and coffee in the lap, laughter, and tears. What has come along with the laughter has been some amazing shared experiences and the creation of new friendships.

Of particular interest is the story of an elderly friend who I had gotten to know over the years. This gentleman was battling late stage cancer. From time to time he would reach out and ask if I would have a moment to speak with him on a topic and I was always better for it. In the summer of 2014 the call came again, but this time it was that I needed to come to lunch to meet someone. "Drew, why don't you come down here on Friday for lunch? I would like you to meet Matt," was the charge. The Friday happened to be the day before Labor Day weekend, and Monterey is a two-hour drive and traffic can be brutal when you are competing with everyone getting out of town.

Regardless, we weren't going anywhere for the weekend and this gentleman was battling cancer and he still was thinking how he could help me. I responded in the affirmative on the spot. The day came and I jumped in my car eager to get to Monterey and also hopeful that I would be back in my car by 2pm. That day at lunch I met a man with whom I ended up working on a large project. He also had driven several hours at our friend's request. Without this lunch, I am sure I would have lived the rest of my life and never met a current work colleague. The memory of his graciousness and connective efforts inspires me.

As we said our goodbyes in the parking lot, our host spoke about how he was moving to a full-time care facility and they had a form for him to fill out. His words still resonate in my mind, *"They had a spot where they wanted you to list hobbies, and I wrote one word. People."*

That friend died a few months later and I am sure I was just one of thousands of people connected by this gentleman in his lifetime. We share our thoughts on lunch for you and your career in honor of him and his legacy. His name you ask? He was loving husband and family man, ardent University of California Golden Bear, and life-long community bank executive, Hugh Barton.

Chapter 2
Setting Up Your System for Success

You need to be able to answer three questions to efficiently set up a business lunch program: whom should I go to lunch with; when should we go to lunch; and why should they say yes to having lunch with me? Understanding the correct answer in each case will allow you to make good choices and build momentum with your new effort. Ideally, you would like to go to lunch with an interesting person that is active in their job and pursuits and discuss their current work projects, and schedule about three weeks out.

Doing this once can take a great deal of effort and appear to be not worth the investment. Setting up a system that identifies people like this, and having a spot on your calendar that is set aside for these lunches, is well worth the effort.

Such a system also produces a constant yield of relevant business information, which can also then be information from your network that may benefit your lunch colleague. When it comes to finding the relevant information about the person you are inviting to lunch, LinkedIn has become a fantastic resource for relevant business topics to discuss.

45-Day Worksheet					BANYAN TREE STRATEGIES
Monday	Tuesday Key Time: 3:00pm	Wednesday Key Time: Noon lunch	Thursday Key Time: AM coffee	Friday Key Time: AM coffee; noon lunch	Top Of Mind List people to meet with by category
	3PM_____	Noon_____	_AM_____	_AM_____ Noon_____	Clients:
	3PM_____	Noon_____	_AM_____	_AM_____ Noon_____	Key Influencers:
	3PM_____	Noon_____	_AM_____	_AM_____ Noon_____	Long Shots:
	3PM_____	Noon_____	_AM_____	_AM_____ Noon_____	Pipeline Movers:
	3PM_____	Noon_____	_AM_____	_AM_____ Noon_____	Extras:
	3PM_____	Noon_____	_AM_____	_AM_____ Noon_____	Themes for the Period and Questions to Ask:

With whom should you dine?

Two paths are possible when answering the question of whom you should ask to lunch. The first is to write down the ten most influential people you have met who would remember your name. Aiming high can have a big impact when you are successful, and we encourage people to do the research to make the lunch worthwhile for your high level contact. The second path takes a little more effort, but also should yield a more consistent number of potential lunch mates.

Step one is to export your email contacts and your LinkedIn connections to a central spreadsheet. In step two, delete any duplicates and update the spreadsheet with the basic information of name, email, and phone number.

Step three includes adding two columns, one marked "value" the other marked "strength." The value column is where you are going to rank your contact by the value they may have to your initiatives, and the strength is where you rank your relationship. In step four give each person a score of 1, 3, or 5, with 1 being the highest.

The magic is not in the spreadsheet set up, it is in the sorting.

Once you have ranked your contacts 1,3,5 by value and strength and then attributed them a 1,2,3,4,5, or 9 for pipeline purposes you will sort by value and this will allow you to focus in on your Value 1's and ignore your Strength 1's with Value 5's

First Name	Last Name	Email	Value	Strength	Pipeline
Billy	Bob	billybob@	1	1	1
Margi	Marge	margi@	1	5	3
Richy	Rich	rich@	3	2	5
jerry	brown	jerryl	1	3	2

Value Rank
1= client assets or prestige would make a big impact
3= would meet our current average client standard
5= would not meet our current average client standard

Strength Rank
1= Strong Relationship
3= Ok Relationship
5= Just getting to know each other

Pipeline
1= POI Person of Interest
2= DI Declared your Intentions
3= KT Kick Tires
4= FK Fill or Kill
5= Client
9= Not a Prospect at this time

In step five sort your contact list by value and strength. Once completed, this two-hour exercise gives you a large list of people whom you can invite to lunch. Once this list exists, you don't have to reinvent the wheel every time you come up for air and think you should be reaching out to people. When you deploy the "coming up for air" strategy, our research shows you have lunch with the same seven people over and over again instead of diversifying with a sound strategy.

> *You are not looking to create a definitive difference between contact A or contact B. This is an exercise that helps you identify the people you know well, but it also does something the first list doesn't. It identifies the diamonds in the rough that you are neglecting.*

Notes:

Chapter 3
Why the Time of Year Makes a Difference

Organizational trainers and behavioral coaches will often back their way into the number of times you should do something, with the assumption that all months, weeks, and days are the same. While the sun may rise in the east and set in the west every day, every professional know certain days of the year are more important than others. Clients and prospects are hard to find in August; are at a party in December; and are laser-focused on work in January.

With this in mind we have developed the 8 x 45-day calendar. It is born from ten years of tracking when people would meet with us, and what the tenor of the conversation was like. The data shows there are three different types of 45-day periods. We will describe them here in "tiers" and refer to them throughout the document.

#	8 x 45 Segments	Tier
1	January 1 – February 15	Tier 1
2	February 15 – April 1	Tier 1
3	April 1 – May 15	Tier 2
4	May 15 – July 1	Tier 2
5	July 1 – August 15	Tier 3
6	August 15 – October 1	Tier 1
7	October 1 – November 15	Tier 1
8	November 15 – January 1	Tier 3

Tier 1 is "peak work season" when everyone has their business hat on and it can be difficult to meet with people because of the increased focus on getting work done. However, lunches during this time can be the most productive, so we focus on the quality of the interaction. Tier 2 we see as "moderate work season," which are transition periods where meetings can be scheduled easily, but may not be as productive as in Tier 1. Finally, in Tier 3 there are the "low work periods," where scheduling a business meeting with a qualified target can be quite challenging as most are on vacation, or are between trips and trying to catch up. Lunches during Tier 3 periods can be long and relaxing, but scheduling them can be difficult.

Changing how you view the calendar will allow you to recognize that it is not feasible to apply an annual goal evenly across 52 weeks.

A uniform, blanket strategy will only lead to frustration. Instead, consider that there are 40 weeks a year which are impactful for most industry segments. Planning ahead, you can deploy your strategy of asking interesting people to lunch at the right time during the key season of their year. Looking back at the original premise that most coaches and trainers espouse, there are clear differences in people's availability and interest in joining you for an open-ended lunch. Plan around these slow times and make sure you aren't resting at the wrong time. You may get a deal on an airline ticket and a condo in Hawaii, but the meetings you are missing back home are costing you thousands.

The previous graphic gives a quick snapshot of the eight segments by tier; on the following pages are some insights into our 8 x 45-day calendar system:

1   January 1 to February 15

Tier 1 (peak work season)
- Within 4 days of New Years, the business world kicks into gear and professionals are back at work and ready to win whatever game they are playing. Lunches at this time of year can be difficult to schedule because people are so focused on getting off to a fast start. With proper planning and a good reputation, you will end up having some excellent conversations and walk away enthused.

Conversation topics
- How were the holidays? How did it go with the relatives? What are the goals for the year ahead?

Veteran's Insight:
- The first week of the year is actually quite open on most people's calendars. Getting on the calendar that last week in December is hard, but you actually can get a rare "are you free today for lunch" success story at this time of year. Don't bank on it, but think about it and have a few targets picked out.

Mood:
- Optimism reigns

② February 16 to April 1

Tier 1 (peak work season)
- The Presidents' birthday holidays float a bit but by mid-Feb many of your targets will have real momentum going and your biggest obstacle during this period will be their travel. We have found this to be a very impactful lunch period, but you have to plan ahead.

Conversation topics
- Skiing, winter break, getaways and how Q1 is shaping up

Veteran's Insight:
- When having a lunch with an influential contact, this is the time of year when they are probably planning something really fun that you may not be able to afford yet. People who plan big trips love to talk about them, so be ready to ask questions.

Mood:
- What are the themes for the year? Are there any new threats to the economy?

③ April 1 to May 15

Tier 2 (moderate work season)
- The start of Q2 and the warmer weather will create a lunch focused on the coming season of summer and also the pending end of school. Lunches are easy to come by in this period, and with the passing of Tax Day many will be looking to talk opportunities for growth.

Conversation topics
- Taxes, baseball, summer plans

Veteran's Insight:
- For many this is the final 45-day period of their real fiscal year. If the money isn't made by this time, they aren't going to find it during the summer. In fact, they spend the summer looking ahead to the next year. Understand the seasons of your contacts and pose your questions correctly and the conversation will flow.

Mood:
- Focused, but ready for the long days of summer

4   May 15 to July 1

Tier 2 (moderate work season)
- We have found the end of May and early June to be a time of great distraction. Your contacts are planning summer vacations. The summer experience of having difficulty finding people in town may start to be a problem, but when you do meet with people, the conversations can be quite varied.

Conversation topics
- What are your summer plans? Is anyone in your extended family off to a new school this fall? How has the first half of the year been?

Veteran's Insight:
- Graduation time makes for easy conversation. If your lunch guest has a child graduating from kindergarten to graduate school, bring it up and watch your friend come to life. This is also a great time of year to ask about future plans as summer leads to contemplation.

Mood:
- Can be distracted and ready for a rest

5   July 1 to August 15

Tier 3 (low work season)
- This is the slowest time of year for most industries unless you run a summer camp. For the rest of us, skinned knees and bug bites from being outdoors are the norm. When people are in town they should have time because the customers are on vacation as well.

Conversation topics
- Stories from time away abound and the ever-nearing fall rush is in the back of everyone's mind.

Veteran's Insight:
- Shoot for the stars at this time of year and, if you need to, throw in a breakfast that is really close to where they live. Even for the titans of industry, the summer slows down and a well-timed request may just land you lunch with a king of the jungle.

Mood:
- Slow

6

August 15 to October 1

Tier 1 (peak work season)
- Welcome back to prime time! With schools pushing their start dates further and further into August, this 45-day period has started to rival the first 45 days of the year for effectiveness and activity. Business can dominate this lunch as plenty of people will have an initiative they would like to accomplish by year's end.

Conversation topics
- What needs to happen by the end of this year? What are you predictions for the football season? How is the weather going to be this fall and winter?

Veteran's Insight:
- When you plan ahead and get your lunches set up early, this can be the best time of year for high impact meals. Plans that seemed far off at the beginning of the year are now front and center. Decision makers will be more apt to move forward.

Mood:
- Focused

7

October 1 to November 15

Tier 1 (peak work season)
- The penultimate 45 days of the year bring some of your best opportunities to talk about the future as it is budget time. Your lunch companions are going to be closing out the year and looking ahead and are in brainstorming mode. What better time to brainstorm than over lunch?

Conversation topics
- Halloween, Thanksgiving and the December holidays. If business relevant, how was the harvest? Now that you have the budget, how are you going to get it done?

Veteran's Insight:
- Your biggest meals of the year happen now. Plan ahead so that you are part of the table discussions and not left on the sidelines.

Mood:
- Tense

8   November 15 to January 1

Tier 3 (low work season)	• The end of the year may appear to be a great business period but in fact most of the high impact lunches have occurred. The business lunch suffers under the weight of work and family parties. A good thing to do with this group of people is to push your lunch date into the next year when everyone is fired up and fresh.
Conversation topics	• How was the year? Being thankful? Honor those who have passed away. Talk about the holiday season excitement of kids and family.
Veteran's Insight:	• You can keep your habits in shape by taking close friends to lunch and a mentor will find the time, but your efforts should be on your year-end action items.
Mood:	• Festive

How to work within "The Magic Window"

Early on in our research we started to notice that while we could sometimes get lucky and find a "next day" lunch, most of our targets were "slammed." When we dug a little deeper what we learned is that slammed or buried was actually only a two-week phenomenon. Most people's calendars start to open up at three weeks out giving you the starting point on the calendar of what we call the "Magic Window." Getting a lunch on the calendar three weeks out on a specific day starts to subtly get the point across that you respect your own time as much as they do theirs. If they can't fit your times, go to the next week. You can do this up to six weeks out without losing effectiveness. Wednesday and Friday at noon are the best hours of the week to shoot for.

We have found this three to six week out period, the "Magic Window" works time and time again. It respects your intended target's time and shows you have a plan for your time as well. When the inevitable "sorry to cancel" email comes as their "slammed" life catches up with them, you get another confidence boost when you offer another date back in the Magic Window. This also presents a calming notion and shows you have a general interest in them. If you had a deal or a sale in mind you would be pressing them for a quicker date. Trust in this process and watch the quality of target you are dining with improve. Use our handy calendar template, or make your own.

Notes:

Chapter 4
Your Lunch Why

Your moment of deep fear is now here. Why should someone say yes to lunch with you? In your world they may be important and may also hold that aura, but somewhere along the way you have a shared experience or know each other, and you are reaching out to build your relationship. You know they are busy, but you have the Magic Window on your side; and with persistence and insight you will find the space in their calendar. But what if they just don't think you are worth it? Can you handle the rejection? This is where having a solid reason why you want to go to lunch can be the bridge to carry you over your valley of fear.

We advise a well-written email that includes several key elements. First, you want to connect into their world and their initiatives. Secondly, you want to elicit their perspective and coaching on **your** initiatives. Finally, you may want to ask for their consideration to partner on a joint initiative. You do not need to include all three of these in your invitation email: people seldom read emails that are too long. What you do need to do is weave your *why* into the *when* and *where* in your email invitation. The higher up the business food chain you are going, the more we suggest taking the "coaching request" route. The more diverse targets will respond well to the "it would be great to learn more about your industry" request. Those that are in your sector and are peers will respond well to the "we may want to put our heads together about partnering in the future" offer.

In summary, the more creative your "why", the better your chance of ending up at lunch with interesting people. The good news is that as you start sending your emails each week inviting someone to lunch, in three weeks you will get better at setting the tone for a safe and fun shared experience, full of energy. Many times during the course of conversation and discussion, you will be amazed to find that you actually do have something to offer to your lunch target.

Picking the right location

One of the benefits of most urban settings is that along with daytime density comes-above average cuisine. Most fine restaurants don't open to serve lunch; they exist to reap the benefits of dinner time. These restaurants know a fantastic lunch will bring people back for dinner with friends hoping they will order wine and dessert. Over half of your targets will have fine cuisine as a "top 3" topic of discussion, and most restaurants offer an excellent lunch for less than $75.

Look at your target area and pick two or three restaurants that most people would consider a good choice for lunch. "Good" means nearly excellent food, but not over-the-top famous or expensive, and has a host or general manager you can get to know.

You don't need to spend a lot of time scoping out the restaurants, and if you have a favorite spot then run with it. The key is you should feel comfortable, and as you start to dine there on a regular basis the owner and servers will recognize you. The recognition comes from your frequency and your openness with those on site, and this pays dividends with your guest. Take a minute now and write out a few spots that come to mind. For example, here in the San Francisco Bay Area it is necessary for people to have several spots based upon geography and traffic patterns. The key is for you to plan ahead and have your lunches add to your work momentum, not detract from it.

The Pre-work: BI-PI-SE

You succeeded and an invitation was accepted. You now have your lunch date set, target acquired and location picked. Now what on earth are you going to talk about? What if they are in a bad mood? Visions of dating disasters linger in the subconscious for most of us. Fear not, most adults have acquired an assemblage of manners and conversational ability. We still recommend you prepare, to become excellent at the business lunch.

The Business Information (BI)

On the Pre-Lunch worksheet in the appendix and on our website, you will see that the Business Information about your guest will be on the web and LinkedIn. Organizing the data on a one-pager, noting college and past companies worked at can be lifesavers over lunch. (Hint: except for engineers, jobs held less than 2 years make for bad subjects or landmines, as seldom do we look to only work somewhere two years.) Other interesting things that can fall under the BI category are charity boards they serve on. These roles are great places to start your conversation.

The Personal Information (PI)

Most people, if you meet them in a conference room, will only share their BI with you. If you make it into their office, it will be almost impossible for you not to pick up some personal information about them, and this can be the next layer of your relational bond. If you meet someone in a social setting, often the BI and the PI are reversed.

You will discuss your family and other personal anecdotes before talking about professional interests. Regardless of how you met them it is vital that you write down prior to the meeting the "PI" that you know so you can see what you don't know.

Personal Information (PI) can be a double-edged sword, as a person who is happy at work may not be so happy at home. Nothing stops the flow of a lunch like asking after a spouse, only to find out they have cancer, have died, or are recently divorced. Children are equally challenging to ask after, as the absence of them or significant issues can be a real source of pain. Family topics and connections can be pursued if the person volunteers the information or opens up the topic.

While the BI and the PI can afford you a few conversational moments the power of a shared experience cannot be underestimated. Shared experiences can be as small as a plane ride in which you sat next to each other, or as big as going to college together. It can also be something you both have done, but not together. You might share the experience of going to the same high school but graduated a decade apart, for instance.

In fact, the magic of 50 lunches is that you are creating new shared experiences that will add up over time and give you a wide scope of people with whom you have good relationships. Shared experiences afford people a window into your character. Once they have a vantage point into your character you have created an opportunity for them to build a personal basis of trust. We believe trust to be a power emotion.

Here's our formula for shared experiences.

$$SE \ (Shared \ Experiences) = C \ (Character) = T \ (Trust)$$
$$= Opportunity. \ In \ short \ form:$$
$$SE = C = T = Opp$$

Once trust is established, all that remains is for the two parties to agree on what they want to transfer between each other. Goods and services, money and recommendations all flow back and forth between trusting parties.

This shared experience formula allows you to enjoy your lunch and realize that as you spend time together the shared experience bonds are forming. As long as you treat the other party well, then you will have at a minimum a new "character" reference. A good lunch together can be that powerful.

Chapter 5
Finally, the Meal

The date you both agreed to is here! You arrive 10 minutes early to check in and greet your guest so you can be seated. The hostess seats you at your table and your napkin goes in your lap. For obvious reasons, the other thing that should be turned off and stowed away is your cell phone. You may want it out until your guest arrives in case they are trying to contact you about being late or are lost, but your focus needs to be on your guest after that.

The good news is that what follows is highly predictable. The restaurant owner and all its employees would like to "turn" the table in 1 hour 15 minutes if not sooner. This consistent and constant force allows you and your guest the comfort of knowing that your meeting has a beginning, middle, and an end. In essence you are renting the table with your meal and beverages. Overseeing the process on behalf of the owner is the waiter.

Body language

Non-verbal communication, or body language is something that does not always get enough attention. It is widely discussed that the younger generation has less awareness or subtlety with the art of body language because of the fact they have grown up with so many other modes of communication like text, email, and social media. If your lunch strategy is to be successful, nailing your non-verbal communication is a key element to developing trust and authenticity with your eating partner. Eye contact, hand movements, facial expressions are very important in conveying how interested you are in engaging with another person. Do not underestimate the ability of your lunch partner, especially if they are older, to hone in on this. You must be fully engaged in this process and not go through the motions. Practice with good friends or your parents or aunts and uncles if this is an area you are not comfortable with.

When you are seated

Once you are seated, you can expect to have the waiter help you get through the meal on a schedule. This is a big help for you as you start taking people to lunch. The first thing you will be asked is if you would like anything to drink. Clearly the restaurant would love you to order alcohol so the bill can go up, but for our purposes we are going to advise you to stick to water, iced tea or a soda of your choice. If your guest starts out with an order of alcohol, it is your call if you would like to follow.

After your drinks are delivered and the conversation has started -- on one of the easy topics already outlined in the 45-day windows -- you will want to give your menu a glance, and if you have a favorite dish you should share that information with your guest. One thing to never share with your guest is your 50 lunches strategy. Nobody wants to part of a strategy or be number 49 with one to go to make your goal. Respect and authenticity should reign supreme.

The waiter will be back shortly after the drinks arrive to inquire about your meal choices. We recommend you have a good dialogue with the waiter and ask their opinion about the specials and their favorite choices. Once you have this flow established, allow your guest to order first and then make your choices.

Veteran's insight
Avoid lunch entrees with sauces and soups. You don't want to end up wearing your meal.

Between ordering and the meal
Now that you have ordered, you will likely have 7 to 12 minutes of uninterrupted time with your guest. This is a perfect time for your first solid question of the lunch. Remember this isn't a sales call and you aren't closing anything. You are exploring their world and learning their perspective, and this is the perfect time to get started.

Veteran's insight
Bread is offered at most restaurants, and sits there just waiting for you to grab a piece. Unless your guest takes a piece, stay away. You don't need it and it's messy.

Food arrives
Your food arriving is a nice break in your dialogue. It allows some natural breaks as you cut and eat. If the first conversation has run its

course, it also allows you to pivot and start down a new path. You have 15 minutes to eat your meal and chances are your waiter will leave you alone or check in once. Use this main chunk of time to introduce a key thought or pose your larger discussion question.

Veteran's insight

The pace at which your guest eats should be something you mirror. It shouldn't be obvious, but finishing your meal before they are halfway through will bring a server to your table to remove your plate and it can be awkward. Seek to be in rhythm with your guest and finish in unison.

Your food is finished

The moment you are finished with the meal, the "busing" team will be on your table like clockwork and your server will inquire about a cup of coffee and dessert. This is a pivotal part of the meal, because your guest's choice will determine if you are wrapping things up or have earned unexpected bonus time. The end of the meal cup of coffee is your cue to keep the dialogue going, and maybe ask one final follow-up question.

Veteran's insight

We suggest you always have an interest in having an end-of-meal coffee, and we advise you always order decaf coffee. You don't want to bully your guest into having coffee, but if you can influence them to do so, it can really have a calming effect on the meal, and provide an opportunity for them to bring your discussions to a close.

The bill

When your guest declines coffee or the coffee is finished, your server is going to bring the bill. We recommend you gently and assertively slide the bill over to yourself and pay with your credit card. If your guest protests loudly that you split the meal, we suggest you consider the request. This is not a good sign and you will want to give them the chance to exit gracefully. In most cases, though, they will offer gently, and you should thank them and then suggest that lunch was your idea and you appreciate them coming and cite something you learned from them. You can then offer a final gesture of suggesting they get the next one, as you really enjoyed the lunch.

Veteran's insight

The goal of the lunch is another interaction at some point. It may be an introduction, another meal, or a meeting. Regardless, your offering to pay is important. Their request to split the bill may be your guest's nuanced way of saying "let's take this slow" and "I don't want to owe you anything."

Chapter 6:
The Follow-Up

You part with smiles and a handshake, both with someone to call or email on behalf of the other. As you walk back to your office or car, the urge to check your phone for that massively important email hits you. RESIST the urge to do this. Take the next 15 minutes and reflect on the meal, the restaurant and the person you had lunch with. Allow your thoughts to settle and get them into your long-term memory. Take a minute and look over your notecard for follow-up. Write down when you will have your items completed. Now you can reengage the Ferris wheel that is your inbox.

Veteran's insight
Within 24 hours send an email with your thoughts and follow-up items listed: we suggest right away for a key follow-up, and within 24 hours for a general "it was good to see you" email.

Congratulations!
You have just created a new shared experience. Most lunches are just stepping stones in a lifetime of network building and friendship. However, reviewed over a 90-day or 180-day period, you will start to notice that when you relate to, reference, or directly talk to someone whom you have lunched with, your communication will change. A friend becomes a good friend, and an acquaintance becomes a friend. As you focus on growing the influence of those around you, your own experiences will be tethered to theirs. Your joint future will be win-win.

Here are some key points to remember when thinking about building your network. First, remember the power of a specific day each week to have lunch with an interesting person. As a reminder, we think Wednesday or Friday at noon are the two most powerful hours of the week. Set the bar low at first by picking out two dates a month and watch how easily it becomes once a week.

Second, leverage the time of year of your lunch to make sure you are meeting with the right people at the right time of year and that you are prepared with the right conversation-inducing questions.

Third, pay attention to the people you are inviting to lunch. Make it easy for them (and you) by planning ahead on the date and the location.

Fourth, recognize the power of a shared working lunch to create a great shared experience. The restaurants need to turn the table enable you to begin and end a meeting; use this to your advantage.

Finally, set your sights on improving the lives of those you are meeting with. Do this through preparation and thinking connectively for them within your network. Most problems are people problems, and most of the time it is because your friend hasn't met the right person. Be an empathetic listener and then when the time is right, offer to help. These introductions will become like the pistons firing in an engine, fueling the progress of your friends who will in turn take the time to care about your goals.

Thinking back, look at whom you ate with in the last 12 months and most likely your influence matches their level. Now look forward 12 months. If you would like to improve your career, or a cause you care about, start by changing the level of the people you are choosing to dine with. Hugh Barton spent a life being interested in "people.". We think this is a great place to start. Send an email to someone you find interesting and somewhere in the email say, "Would you like to go to lunch?" **Go for it.**

Appendix

Banyan Tree Strategies
Templates

1. 45-Day Worksheet
2. 45-Day Follow-Up Questions
3. Wedding Cake Layers (2 pages)
4. Interesting Things Worksheet
5. Pre-Lunch Worksheet
6. Overall Task List
7. Prioritizing Tasks
8. Personal Goal and Behavior Sheet
9. Value Rank Contacts Sample
10. Mapping Your Boss

**Templates also available to download at full size
at www.banyantreestrategies.com/publications**

45-Day Worksheet

BANYAN TREE STRATEGIES

Monday	Tuesday Key Time: 3:00pm	Wednesday Key Time: Noon lunch	Thursday Key Time: AM coffee	Friday Key Time: AM coffee; noon lunch	Top Of Mind List people to meet with by category
	3PM ___	Noon ___	AM ___	AM ___ Noon ___	Clients:
	3PM ___	Noon ___	AM ___	AM ___ Noon ___	Key Influencers:
	3PM ___	Noon ___	AM ___	AM ___ Noon ___	Long Shots:
	3PM ___	Noon ___	AM ___	AM ___ Noon ___	Pipeline Movers:
	3PM ___	Noon ___	AM ___	AM ___ Noon ___	Extras:
	3PM ___	Noon ___	AM ___	AM ___ Noon ___	Themes for the Period and Questions to Ask:

45-Day Follow-Up Questions

1. What positive things happened to you in the last 45 days?

2. What distracted you in the last 45 days?

3. What needs to happen in the next 45 days?

4. Prioritize your follow-up behavior for the next 45 days:

Wedding Cake Exercise – Write In Your Value Layers

What does SUCCESS look like here?

90 Days:

1 Year:

3 Years:

5 Years:

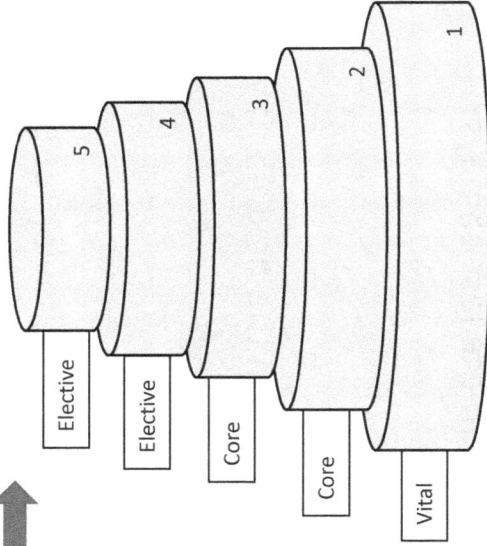

Cake Layer samples:

Work, Health/Fitness, Faith, Fun/Recreation, Family/Relationships, Community Service

Questions to fill in on next page

- What behaviors are you going to STOP?

- What behaviors are you going to START?

- Whom do you need to STOP emulating?

- Whom do you need to START emulating?

- Identify the Key People you can share your plan with

- Identify the people whom you may upset with your change

45-Day Follow Up Worksheet – Cake Layers

1	2	3	4	5

Interesting Things With Interesting People....

THE CASUAL MEETING: Send an email "good to see you."

1.

2.

3.

Notes:

YOU-HIT-IT-OFF MEETING: Send a "good to see you" along with an "I had a thought for you based on our conversation," and also perhaps suggest you introduce them to someone that might interest them.

1.

2.

3.

Notes:

SPARKS-WERE-FLYING ENCOUNTER: Send an email to follow up suggesting lunch or coffee.

1.

2.

3.

Notes:

Notes:

Pre-Lunch Worksheet

Who:

What They Do:

What They Are Great At:

Their Top Rocks:	People They Know on LinkedIn That Might Be Interesting to You:
1.	1.
2.	2.
3.	Your Impending Events:
Do They Have a Bumper Sticker Issue?	1.
1.	2.
People You Know That Might Be Able to Help Them:	Who Have You Met With in the Last Two Weeks Who Was Interesting?
1.	1.
2.	2.
3.	3

Notes:

Overall Task List

BANYAN TREE STRATEGIES

List your To-Dos in no particular order

Prioritizing

A High Priority	Est. Time	B Medium Priority	Est. Time	C Low Priority	Est. Time
Fire Drills:					

Value Rank Contacts - Sample

The magic is not in the spreadsheet set up, it is in the sorting.

Once you have ranked your contacts 1,3,5 by value and strength and then attributed them a 1,2,3,4,5, or 9 for pipeline purposes you will sort by value and this will allow you to focus in on your Value 1's and ignore your Strength 1's with Value 5's

First Name	Last Name	Email	Value	Strength	Pipeline	Value Rank
						1= client assets or prestige would make a big impact
Billy	Bob	billybob@	1	1	1	3= would meet our current average client standard
Margi	Marge	margi@	1	5	3	5= would not meet our current average client standard
Richy	Rich	rich@	3	2	5	
jerry	brown	jerry!	1	3	2	
						Strength Rank
						1= Strong Relationship
						3= Ok Relationship
						5= Just getting to know each other
						Pipeline
						1= POI Person of Interest
						2= DI Declared your Intentions
						3= KT Kick Tires
						4= FK Fill or Kill
						5= Client
						9= Not a Prospect at this time

Notes:

Notes:

The Next Gen Almanac
Mapping Your Boss

NOTES

✓ **Extrovert or Introvert?**
- ☐ Extrovert
- ☐ Introvert

✓ **Reader or Listener?**   **Tip:** Watch how they order food from a restaurant.
- ☐ Reader
- ☐ Listener

✓ **Morning or Evening Person?**   **Tip:** Look for when emails come from them.
- ☐ Morning
- ☐ Evening

✓ **What types of teams or performers do they like?**
1.
2.
3.
4.

✓ **Do they identify with a certain culture in a major way? If so, the codes of behavior from that culture will matter a lot to them. For example: Baseball guys typically have an "unwritten" code that you either get or don't get and you only get it by studying the game.**
1.
2.
3.
4.

✓ **What stories do they tell about success? They will want to relive those stories with your team.**
1.
2.
3.
4.

✓ **If they were a superhero, which superhero would they be?**
1.